4X4 OFFROAD RACING TRUCKS

Bill Holder and John Carollo
Foreword by Rod Hall

Iconografix

Iconografix
PO Box 446
Hudson, Wisconsin 54016 USA

Library of Congress Control Number: 2009930372

ISBN-13: 978-1-58388-243-6
ISBN-10: 1-58388-243-X

09 10 11 12 13 6 5 4 3 2 1

Printed in China

Cover and book design by Dan Perry

Copyedited by Andy Lindberg

On the cover: Left: Off Road race trucks provide plenty of excitement from getting airborne jumping small and large drops to racing side by side, all while sliding on dirt or mud.

Middle: The popularity of diesel truck pulls is growing rapidly. Seeing everything from a slightly modified street truck to over the top purpose built race trucks is always punctuated by the plume of thick black smoke they spew under load.

Right: Churning all four tires into the loose dirt surface, this Off Road racer is making time by sliding his truck through a turn. It's a controlled slide, often maneuvered by only the gas pedal.

TABLE OF CONTENTS

ACKNOWLEDGEMENTS

1. Jimmy Greaves, CORR
2. Wesley Harmon, CORR
3. Patricia Williams, MDR
4. Steve Weiss, WSORR
5. Bob Sayers, WSORR
6. Ken Leavitt, SNORE
7. The Promotions Company — Family Events

FOREWORD BY ROD HALL
(LEGENDARY NATIONAL OFF-ROAD RACER)

Recreational four-wheeling got its start after WWII when thousands of men returned home from war. There was a huge surplus of Jeeps that were being purchased by veterans who had developed an expertise in the use of 4x4s during the war.

In the mid-1950s, clubs were forming and creating a variety of organized events for off-road enthusiasts. I bought my first worn-out jeep in 1956 and went four-wheeling. As interest developed, aftermarket companies were being formed to provide parts for the 4x4 high-performance market.

The first organized off-road event was the Afton Canyon Junket, which I won in 1964. Then, off-road racing began on a regular basis for me in 1967, and 40 years later, I am still racing stock production 4x4 vehicles. In 2007, I won my 19th Baja 1000 driving a 4x4 HUMMER H3 and also have a record of 18 Baja 500 wins.

In the beginning, there were mostly production-based vehicles ranging from 2WD cars, 2WD pickups, 4x4 pickups, buggies, and motorcycles. Today, off-roading is multifaceted from recreational family four-wheeling to many forms of extreme competition. Off-roading in its many forms continues to be a thriving and growing industry.

I have always raced 4x4 vehicles and I sometimes ask the 2WD racers, "How was it out there when you were stuck and only had half a truck?"

Rod Hall

When one mentions 4x4 Off-Road Trucks, photos like this probably come to mind. The air is filled with swirling dust and dirt clods, almost completely obscuring visibility and making it rough for drivers and fans alike.

INTRODUCTION

Trucks have become a happening through the recent decades with more than half of the vehicles sold being those working vehicles. With their rugged macho appearances, they seem to be pleading for competition. And when you view the contents of this book, you will certainly see that is the case. To realize the ultimate potential of a competitive truck, many of the off-road activities fit well with four-wheel-drive trucks. These are the vehicles that will be addressed here.

Loyal truck owners and race fans across the country get healthy doses of truck racing and other competitions everywhere they look. Appealing to a wideband truck audience, trucks compete in many types of motorsports where no car would dare show its face. The popular-ity of the four-wheel off-road sport can be seen by the exposure it gets on national TV with a number of the different dirt activities televised on a regular basis.

Look at the details and emblems that are now appearing on new pickup trucks. Statements like "Z71 Off Road," "Off Road 4 Wheel Drive," and "TRD Off Road" have obvious off-road implications. Also, Mickey Thompson Tires features a deep-treaded model called "Baja Belted."

There's nothing like the sight of four heavy-lugged tires clawing for traction and throwing up clouds of dirt and rocks. That's not totally complete, though, as competition 4WD trucks also compete in mud, salt, and sand.

Of course, when truck racing is mentioned, probably the most vivid pictures of trucks in flight are at the famous super-long desert off-road encounters, which often stretch out hundreds of miles. This competition is also done worldwide with the most famous being the tortuous Dakar Rally.

There is also closed-course racing which is basically an oval version of the desert racing. It provides considerably more side-by-side racing with significant contact often resulting with body sheet metal being shredded or torn off.

Also, for what is called "Obstacle Course" racing, it is necessary for the trucks to navigate courses with jumps, water, and other tough areas to pass through. There are a number of different names for this type of competition with "Tough Trucks" probably being the most popular.

Probably the most recognized trucks doing this type of obstacle four-wheel off-roading are the big-wheeled Monster Trucks. Talk about air time, you really get it from these giant yet amazingly agile machines.

Drag racing of several different types is a part of the motorsports agenda of trucks. First, there is the high-speed sand dragging which is very applicable for these four-wheel drive trucks. Making it a little tougher, there are the up-hill drags which provide a tougher test for the powertrains. Then, there is mud dragging, a totally different situation where the oozy goo is trying to bring those big tires to a stop.

Taking the up-hill drags one step further are the so-called hill climbs. The most famous is the Pikes Peak Hill Climb. Although there aren't many, there are some four-wheel-drive trucks that challenge land speed records on the salt.

Other off-road motorsports attempt to impede progress. Four-wheel-drive pulling trucks try to pull thousands of pounds three hundred feet from a dead stop.

Then, there is the ultra-slow truck motorsports activity called rock-climbing. This involves trying to get over the toughest of obstacles requiring a delicate touch on the throttle and a skilled use of the suspension system. A similar activity is the Trail Riding event that combines a number of rock-climbing obstacles over the length of an off-road trail.

The ultimate modern-day 4x4 Off-Road Truck is the awesome High Mobility Multi-Purpose Wheeled Vehicle (HMMWV) most commonly known as the HumVee or Hummer. This is the military version used by the Army and Marines.

Probably the most-famous off-road race in the world is the Baja 1000 event. The name generates immediate recognition so it's not that surprising that it's used on modern pickup trucks. The Baja name is prominently displayed on this Chevy S-10 pickup.

For the young of age, and even some adults, the popular off-road truck has also made itself felt in miniature with radio-controlled models. These sophisticated models are equally exciting, only at a smaller scale! Whatever the use, racing 4X4 trucks is fun for young and old.

The 'Off-Road' name has also found its way onto the sheet metal of modern pickups. Notice on the maroon-background photo that a mountain range is shown behind the off-road lettering indicating a hill-climbing capability.

Trail riding is an increasingly popular off-road activity in this country, requiring a 4x4 truck or vehicle and a skilled driver. These BF Goodrich tires were designed specifically for that challenging activity.

Traction is everything in four-wheeling. In sand dragging and hill climbing, paddle tires like this are sometimes used. The paddles are actually vulcanized onto slicks and dig into the dirt or sand like a power shovel.

The off-road sport is also a great influence on certain modified pickup trucks. These two trucks certainly show that influence in a big way. Note the high stance of each. Strength is also a characteristic of these trucks with that sturdy tubular frame on the gray truck. With the off-road look usually comes big power under the hood.

Can trucks fly? If you are driving a high-performance 4x4 Off-Road Truck, you better believe that you can! As you can see, this truck is flying high off the top of a hill, but it has the suspension system to absorb the shock of impact.

The fury of off-road racing is also evident in the powered model truck hobby. Looking at these two model off-roads makes it hard to discern whether they are real or a model. There are 4x4 models with gas, battery, or electric engines. That is the Scorpion Rock Climber on the left while the T-Maxx Monster Truck is below.

A little traction please! And that is certainly being applied by this four-wheel-drive Dodge Ram pickup. From the dust patterns, it is easy to see that significant contributions are being made by both front and rear wheels.

CHAPTER 1: DESERT AND CLOSED COURSE RACING

When many racing fans think about competition pickups, a large number will think about the grueling test pickups face running for hundreds of miles across the desert in such famous races as the Baja 1000. In more subtle applications, pickups have also competed on shorter off-road courses and even inside stadiums.

Desert Racing — Perhaps the ultimate test to pickups in competition is the bumpy, dusty, hours-long races across the deserts of the southwestern United States. The distances of these grueling affairs are as long as a thousand miles. Many truck companies sponsor factory teams in these international competitions. And with

successes come national-level advertisements, which flaunt the strength and endurance of a particular brand of pickup. Much of the experience that comes from these events serves as research and development for development of the pickup trucks of the future.

With the punishment the trucks endure racing from high altitudes to sea level, through wind and rain, over boulders and ravines, every part and piece of every truck is stressed to the ultimate. And it goes without saying that the drivers face the same punishment. Two of the big names in this sport have been Ivan Stewart of the Toyota Team and Walker Evans who runs Dodges.

The two major organizations in promoting these des-

Gustova Vildosola wheels his 4x4 Baja Protruck at the 2005 Baja 1000. This portion of the Baja route is pretty smooth, but that's certainly not the case with much of the course.

ert shows are the SCORE (Southern California Off Road Enthusiasts) and BITD (Best in the Desert) groups.

SCORE — This group was formed in 1973 and today is rated one of the top off-road racing groups. It has concentrated on the long-distance events with races of 500 and a thousand miles in length. The group's top class is the Trophy Cup Class for unlimited production trucks such as Chevy Trailblazers and Ford F150s. Both two- and four-wheel-drive trucks participate. But there are other classes where 4WD Trucks participate.

One of the pioneers of the desert truck racing sport is Rod Hall. He has driven everything through the years, but today concentrates on 4WD production trucks, namely the Hummer. Rod laughed when he explained, "Four wheeling is where I am. Two-wheel drive? Why would I want to drive half a truck?" Rod has been entered in the SCORE-promoted Baja 1000 since 1969! He concentrates on the three classes of the Hummer, H-1, H-2, and H-3, and there's certainly no mistaking these unique machines.

One of the biggest winners in SCORE four-wheel competition is Don Moss who has 29 wins and five championships in Class III, which features short-wheelbase four-wheel-drive trucks.

Driver Rod Hall has been called Mr. Baja for many years. In recent years, he has run the Baja 1000 in a number of factory Hummer 4x4 vehicles. There were three different Hummer versions that he ran. The red vehicle was an H-2 that ran in the 2006 Vegas-to-Reno desert race. The Blue H-3 Hummer is shown competing in the Parker 400 in 2006. The yellow Hummer H-1 is shown racing the Vegas-to-Reno Race in 2007.

Moss's longstanding machine is a '79 Ford Bronco with a pretty-much stock suspension. It carries a 351 Windsor Ford V-8 engine capable of about 350 horsepower. To take care of the ups-and-downs of the courses it traverses, the front shocks have 11 inches of play while in the rear it's an amazing 17 inches.

BITD — There are several classes that allow four-wheel trucks in the BITD (Best in the Desert) organization, Class 7 and 7S. Class 7 allows unlimited mini or mid-size trucks. The six-cylinder engine size is limited to 4.5 liters and the wheelbase must be within two inches of stock. The wheel travel is up to 26 inches in front and almost three feet in the rear. The cost to build one of these trucks starts at about $60,000 with a top speed of 120 miles per hour. The Class 7S trucks are less modified and can be built for $20,000 and have a top speed of about 100 miles per hour.

Stadium Truck Racing — When you mention truck racing, one name keeps coming to the top, that of the late Mickey Thompson. The racer and innovator came up with the idea for racing trucks inside stadiums in a most interesting way. "Back in 1970s, I was truck racing in the desert and having a great wheel-to-wheel competition," said the late Thompson. "We kept passing each other back and forth, time after time. But the only observers were the rattlesnakes and rabbits. Since I figured that somebody would like to see that type of racing up close, I came up with the idea of an indoor truck racing series." Did he ever, and the Mickey Thompson series through the 1980s and 1990s was hugely popular. Thompson came up with some innovative techniques of indoor track building to opti-

The number 300 Ford Bronco desert-racing truck of veteran Don Moss is a regular desert competitor. From this photo, it looks like he's ready to make a four-point landing. This action occurred in the 2008 Baja 1000.

mize safety and competition. The success of the series came down to the fact that there were a number of big-time drivers—with the likes of the Mears Brothers—and a tremendous involvement from the truck companies. Interestingly, there was a greater foreign corporate interest in the series with factory supported Toyota, Mazda and Nissan. US trucks, which had no factory support, carried the Chevy and Ford nametags. It would lead to the popular closed-course racing of today where desert-type racing is carried out in front of crowds who can see the entire course.

Closed Course Racing:

CORR — The evolution of the Mickey Thompson series was the CORR (Championship Off-Road Racing) series, which was formed in the late 1990s. The series has benefited recently from SPEED, and more recently, NBC TV coverage. It has national sponsorship from Lucas Oil Products. CORR runs a number of laps around man-made, off-road courses (the longest being about two miles) with a flock of trucks challenging each other in wheel-to-wheel competition. All the races are in California. The top class is the so-called Pro-4 Class that features four-wheel-drive trucks. These Pro Trucks show big time horsepower and the ability to corner at high speeds. Lots of jumps and tough obstacles require these trucks to be tough as nails.

Johnny Greaves is one of the series' heavy hitters, driving his flashy Monster Energy Toyota four-wheeler. He has won the Pro-4 championship three times and is always running up front. These two-ton trucks are killer-performance machines with some 700 horsepower under the hood. The main brands that participate in this series include Toyota, Ford and Nissan.

WSORR — Another series, the WSORR (World Series of Off-Road Racing), is very similar to CORR with some drivers racing in both of the series. Its top four-wheel class is called the Pro 4x4 Class.

SNORE - The SNORE (Southern Nevada Off-Road Enthusiasts) group runs six or seven races a year mostly in the Las Vegas area. The events run on single laps at 45–60 miles per hour. Its longest race is the SNORE 250, a race that has been contested for over 35 years.

The SNORE Class III Pro 4x4 SWB class features four-wheel-drive trucks. Ken Leavitt is one of the stars of the class, driving his 1985 Ford Bronco that shows over 15,000 miles. It has 14 inches of shock travel in the front and 20 in the rear. Weighing in at about 4,300 pounds, Leavitt has about $30,000 in the machine.

MDR — The MDR (Mojave Desert Racing) group has seven closed-course truck classes. The Formula 4x4 Class is the only pure four-by-four class that uses production trucks with more than five thousand being built. An example of one of these trucks is that of Bob Sayers' Ford Bronco. With a 410-cubic-inch V-8 under the hood, the 3800-pound truck is capable of 120–130 mile per hour speeds.

But the point must be made that the national groups are not the only game in town as far as closed-course racing is concerned. At a number of locations around the country, there are closed-course races where amateur teams can participate.

No fancy crew uniforms for the Moss Racing Team. They would probably get dirty if they had them. Even with all the hazards the truck races on desert courses, Moss says a set of off-road tires last him for two seasons!

Truck staging for the Baja 1000. There is no way the field could start together, so the starts are staggered, with one truck leaving at a time with a time delay before the next truck gets underway.

The action in the Mickey Thompson series was fast and furious as shown here. Thompson used special walls to try to contain the roaring trucks within the prescribed course route.

An experiment by former desert racer Mickey Thompson during the 1980s led to the closed-course racing. Thompson devised indoor courses with a number of obstacles to negotiate. It was very popular with the public.

Running a 4x4 off-road truck on the desert floor requires carrying as much as possible to repair the truck on the course. If it's too bad, the crew will have to come out and repair it, sometimes losing hours and any chance of winning.

The Baja 1000 is an ultimate challenge. Moss explained, "There are both man-made booby traps and national hazards." He explained that the two-man crew switched off driving every four or five hours.

Since desert racing often includes racing at night, proper lighting is a necessity. Just check out the candlepower of this truck with the powerful beams shining forward, five on the grille and five on the roof.

SCORE is normally known as a point-A-to-point-B group, but on occasion it runs a closed-course event. The close competition of one of those races is shown by this action photo.

This Off Road racer is a mini truck and is prepared for just about every kind of racing. Note the windshield wiper and auxiliary headlights on the front bumper bar. Some desert races often take place through the night and the truck's rack of special made lights are the only source of light.

The patriotically painted off-road truck of Gary Vosburg pours on the coal during a Best In The Desert race. It's clear to see that the four-wheel drive system is working hard as evidenced by the dust boiling up from the two left-side tires.

This off-road truck, driven by Larry Roaeler and Mike Ruane, flies through the air with the greatest of ease. Note that the suspension system is allowing the wheels to hang amazingly low beneath the truck. This action occurred in a Best In The Desert sanctioned race.

A huge American flag frames the off-road Ford truck of Chris Golding and Randy Merritt. The truck was competing in the 8100 Class of a Best In The Desert cross-country race.

You don't normally find a water hazard in a desert race, but that's the case in this BITD race. This is certainly a vivid example of a 4x4 off-road truck's capabilities all working to perfection.

In desert races, it's not all flat terrain to negotiate. There are often irregularities as shown here. The grooved dirt road shows that there has been considerable traffic before this four-wheeler made its trip in a BITD race.

A head-on shot of this BITD truck shows the protection that has been added to the front of the truck. There are vertical bars in front of the radiator with triangular end pieces. Also, there is a sturdy support bar splitting the windshield area.

In this CORR competition, Johnny Greaves in the near truck is hitting the ground just ahead of his chaser. These trucks are built to take such impacts with their custom shock absorbers.

You don't normally think that heavy competition trucks can fly, but this CORR truck certainly disproves that theory. Notice how the rear end is hanging down far below the wheel-well openings.

With the short closed courses that CORR runs, it's very common to have serious contacts between the trucks. This truck had its complete rear sheet metal removed in such a confrontation.

Johnny Greaves' CORR truck appears to be riding the top rail of a grandstand. That's an illusion, of course, but this racing is run very close to the fans on its closed courses. Its format is perfect for live national telecasts.

Protection is just as important in closed-course racing as it is in desert racing. Here, crisscrossing bars protect the front of the radiator. It also provides protection to the radiator in a front-end collision with another truck.

This photo shows a typical engine installation of a CORR closed-course off-road truck. These engines are serious race engines and capable of huge horsepower from their physical small-block V-8 size.

As can be seen in the driver's compartment of this particular CORR truck, there aren't any extras or frills. It's all done in no-nonsense, bare metal with an extra-sturdy racing seat.

One of the biggest names in Off-Road Racing is Walker Evans who has driven in many venues including the SCORE and SODA organizations. He was also a 4x4 truck driver for CORR and won the group's Pro-4 Championship in 1999.

This vintage 4x4 Jeep pickup pulls a hard left turn on an unidentified closed short course. No problem identifying this truck as a four-wheeler as the front differential is clearly visible on the right end of the front axle. Also visible are front parallel leaf springs.

This classy Ford off-road truck is shown in short course competition during the mid-1980s. Even with its height off the racecourse, the truck's heavy-duty suspension system is more than capable of setting it down cleanly.

The clue that this 4x4 Off-Road truck is competing in a local closed course comes from the fact that its hand-painted number sign is duct-taped onto the truck. It, however, certainly doesn't decrease the level of competition on the track.

A Ford (L) and a Chevy duel for position on a closed course. The fact that the factory brands are competing against each other makes these lower level races of great interest to the fans in the stands.

A Tough Truck competitor takes the first ramp of the Obstacle Course. Note the crowds jammed in place to watch. Tough Truck action is just as popular as Monster Trucks as both are often contested in the same show.

CHAPTER 2: OBSTACLE COURSE RACING

While it may sound like a bad day at boot camp, running an obstacle course with a 4X4 has an entirely new meaning. The best part about Obstacle Course Racing is the variety of courses and trucks that run this type of racing.

Tough Truck racing consists of a course laid out for trucks to run one at a time, against the clock. The idea is that all competitors are running the same course, under the same conditions and the times will show who got around the course in the best time to be the winner in his class.

The details are that the courses are laid out to be TOUGH. They try a driver's mettle, his or her truck, and are VERY entertaining and FUN for both viewers and participants alike. Usually set in the infield of a track

or a safe, wide-open area, most Tough Truck courses almost always contain a number of jumps, dips, turns and sometimes even a mud pit. It is up to the competitors to decide just how hard to hit those jumps and dips, power through those turns and how fast to take the mud pit. The entertainment value usually happens when drivers overestimate the quality of both their driving ability and the suspension and handling capabilities of their trucks. Those overdriving either their truck's or their own ability will often be seen 'eating the steering wheel' upon landing, much to the crowd's delight. And Tough Truck courses are never set up the same for an event. Even in the case of a show being a regularly scheduled event, held every year, the show's organizers will make sure the

Tough Truck course is different from the last time it was held there and different from the previous event on the schedule.

Tough Trucks usually race in one of two classes, Stock or Modified. Stock trucks are usually daily drivers with little or no serious modifications and race for trophies and the applause (or hoots and hollers) of the crowd. Modified trucks are usually the ones that follow the series from event to event and these trucks are closer to fully professional race trucks with serious suspension and engine work.

Tough Trucks are, along with Monster Trucks, often the crowd's favorites. In the case of the Monster Trucks, it's the sheer size and power of these beasts. In the case of Tough Trucks, it's the high-flying antics of both the pro racer and the raw newbie trying to counteract the forces of nature.

Monster Trucks run obstacle courses and the biggest difference is when you are driving a Monster Truck, there aren't too many things that can be an effective obstacle. So show promoters and even the Truck teams are always coming up with new things for the big boys of 4X4 racing to run over, destroy and generally beat to a pulp. Have an RV trailer you no longer need? A boat that's not seaworthy? Or how about six junk cars stacked up in a pyramid? None of these are a problem for a Monster Truck and the fans love it when they prove it.

As the drivers do more and more with their vehicles with faster speeds and higher jumps, the realm of danger increases greatly. Modern Monster Trucks are outfitted with safety kill switches and some even with remote switches so that should a Monster Truck go out of control, it can be stopped by series officials before it does any damage.

It almost defies physics that a truck weighing close to 10,000 lb. can leap over a stack of cars and plow through an RV trailer with ease, but Monster Trucks are evolutionary creations that keep doing more and doing it better. They started in the 1960s, the results of investigating the results of suspension and tire size changes for increased off-road performance. The pioneer in those investigations was Bob Chandler who worked on

Think Monster Truck suspensions don't need a lot of 'travel'? Check out this shock absorber and note first how long it is and how much travel it has to work on a Monster Truck.

changes to his personal truck. His suspensions kept getting more and more sophisticated and the tires bigger and bigger. And as it would prove out in the years to come, Bob Chandler had created a monster (in physical size, cost, technology, and later in money-making) crowd-pleaser. Today, his Bigfoot trucks continue to be the most famous of the Monster Trucks.

Much like Tough Trucks, a timed run through the Obstacle Course is one way to race a Monster Truck. But many shows have gone to Twin Courses which is two courses virtually identical. That way, TWO Monster Trucks can race each other head-to-head and double the excitement.

This Toyota Tough Truck competitor seems to have the best line off the ramp. Racers and fans know the best way around the track is to be smooth and consistent, and a good ramp launch will help that.

A panel truck body on this competitor doesn't seem to slow it down. As in the case of most types of race vehicles, it's more about the chassis than the body.

The Afterburner Ford takes a ramp with just the right attitude. For Tough Trucks competition, the takeoff is just as important as the landing as doing one or both wrong will cost precious time.

A smooth and consistent line over a ramp ensures a good time for this competitor and it takes both a good suspension and driver to nail down that elusive good time.

You can see the suspension clearance on this Ford Ranger and that is a very important aspect of any type of Off-Road racing. The suspension needs clearance to get across the minor hills and holes of the racing surface.

A Chevy S-10 hits the ramp at speed. Proper gearing puts the engine's RPMs at the disposal of the driver and he or she can time their acceleration to hit a ramp just right.

A Monster Truck wheelie is most impressive when one thinks of just how much power it takes to lift up the entire front end of a 10,000 lb. vehicle and those big wheels and tires.

But sometimes wheelies don't turn out the way the driver planned. This driver lost a wheel upon landing and rolled over. The driver said he knew he "wasn't going to drive out of this one" and was OK.

It takes a big tow truck to move a Monster Truck after an on-track mishap. Here, they are moving the Monster after a rollover was caused by a broken suspension piece

The Raminator gets 'Big Air' off one of the jumps on a monster obstacle course. Like any Off-Road racer that takes a jump or a ramp, it's all about hitting the ramp just right.

The Raminator takes down a stack of hapless cars. Monster Trucks (and their fans) love to crush cars even when they are stacked up. In this case, the top car was thrown by the impact.

Bigfoot, the king of the Monster Trucks, cracks a wheelie off a jump. Using a ramp or jump to start off a wheelie is not always necessary, but it does make it easier for the driver as the truck's weight is transferred during a jump.

Bob Chandler's Bigfoot Ford truck takes off from a jump. For the legions of sometimes-crazy fans, Bigfoot is the granddaddy of Monster Trucks. Bigfoot is the original Monster Truck and has had many incarnations.

A typical Monster Truck engine. This one is a Ford with a supercharger and two big four-barrel carbs. In the past, engines for Monsters were detuned drag engines. Now they use all-out race motors.

When you see eerie red glowing head-lights — sometimes coming right at you — it can only be the famous Grave Digger. The very popular Monster Truck always performs with his red headlights on and…

…keeps them lit while racing. The distinctive red headlights make it a huge favorite with kids and adults alike. The body is based on an early '50s Chevy panel wagon.

The Digger goes for big air and gets it. Grave Digger drivers have a reputation to uphold and never let their many fans down. You can always count on a great performance from the Grave Digger!

This roadster hits the ramp just right. Roadster trucks and others with no roof allow fans to see the driver more clearly as he or she works the steering wheel.

Two clean and ready-to-go Tough Trucks will take the green flag looking neat and clean. Odds are they won't finish their laps the same way. Between dirt and often mud, the trucks will bring some of the racecourse home with them.

A military camo paint scheme is always popular with 4X4 trucks. It ties back to hunting and the ever-popular military theme where many think the sport of Off-Roading originally came.

The Mac Attack Ford running over a small ramp. Note skid pan under front of engine. Skid pans protect the underside of the motor when the suspension travel bottoms out on a hard landing.

They come to the track all clean and neat. They probably won't return home that way. They often wear the mud and dirt like a badge of courage or, at the very least, fun.

This Tough Truck is for longer races and even night events with the extra lights. Note the skid pan on the front. It's better to bounce off of that than the front end of the truck and possibly go end over end.

Off-Road equipment manufacturers know the value of sponsoring racecars for their customers. It means paying customers will want the parts that run well and win for their own trucks.

It may look like a big mess, but it's flat-out fun for the driver. Off-Road racers embrace the dirt and mud as it's part of the fun and attraction.

A full size Ford skates over a small ramp without losing a beat. Having the right suspension parts and setting them all up correctly comes together in places like this.

This heavy Chevy sports a cow paint job. Some teams want to be distinctive, and unique paint is a quick way to attract attention. That is, until the mud starts flying.

Things can get crowded out there pretty fast. As in many other forms of racing, it's the same small piece of real estate that all the racers fight over and only one can win it.

The TowaSaurus Wrex beats down some cars. The Monster Truck took the two highly popular aspects of dinosaurs and Monster Trucks and made a machine that definitely attracts kids' attention.

When a 10,000 lb. Monster Truck rolls over, it's a big deal. In this case, the driver was OK and ended up talking to the track announcer after the scary incident.

Here is the same Monster Truck without many of its body panels. Note the beefy roll cage. The body is more a collection of fiberglass panels than strong sheetmetal pieces such as fenders and doors.

Monster Trucks use steering on all four wheels and that allows them to compensate for being such a big machine. That steering allows the 'big boys' to perform in smaller indoor shows.

You need a tall ladder to work on the biggest of the Bigfoot Monster Trucks. The height came from the big tires and as tires got bigger, so did the trucks.

Like any other racer, you have to work on them. The engine, driveline and chassis all have areas that need maintenance between races to ensure they will perform to their max and be safe and reliable.

Big trucks need big rig haulers but Monster Trucks are taller than the haulers. Teams change tires to lower the heights of the trucks so they will fit into the trailers.

The man who started it all in Monster Trucks, Bob Chandler, creator of Bigfoot. Bob still oversees the many versions of the world's most famous and King of the Monster Trucks.

The Monsters get ready to go out and play. Lining them up right in front of the fans lets the crowd see them up close. And when they fire up, the fans can often literally feel the trucks move the earth.

Kids just love to see Monster Trucks up close. Bring a camera and get the famous, 'My kid is smaller than the wheel' picture. It's also a great time to talk to the drivers and crews.

The Bigfoot Shuttle proves you can make a Monster Truck out of Mom's mini van. We bet this mini van could park anywhere it wanted when shopping at the mall.

The Black Stallion clears another obstacle. Its distinctive name and paint scheme allows fans to associate with it closely and actually build a bond with the team. This 'branding' makes for better sales of team and sponsor merchandising.

Bigfoot V takes on the mud and wins. Was there ever any doubt? As the original Monster Truck, Bigfoot drivers have a good idea what they can to with the 10,000 lb. Ford truck.

This Ford truck shows the right attitude for taking a small ramp on his run. Note how they cleaned only the truck's Super Truck name and logo and the two panels on the hood from the last race's dirt and dust.

After tagging a hay bale and getting airborne, this obstacle racer will have to make up that time. In single truck competition, it's all about the lap times. With multiple truck racing, it's all about leading the pack at the finish line.

Half the fun of a mud pit is that pretty much anyone can try it. Mud racing is not limited to hard core racing machines. You can take your own truck or Jeep and give it a try.

CHAPTER 3: DRAG RACING

The drag racing premise is simple. One or two cars race in a straight line over a measured distance. But 4X4 off-road racers have it all over their pavement competitors. In pavement drag racing, there are only two sizes of tracks, quarter and eighth mile, and only one surface for variety. For 4X4 racers there is more variety and the racers are built for the many types of tracks found. One would think there couldn't be that many types of tracks but there are. Mud, sand and dirt drags start off flat, straight-line racing for 4X4s.

Racing in mud is often called Mud Bog Racing and consists of an actual pit of very wet mud. Earthmovers will make the pit by mounding up four walls in a rectangular pattern. Once the walls are complete, the water truck stops by and unloads thousands of gallons of water in the center of the pit. The water mixes with the dirt and mud is created. Add a 4X4 with big tires to act as the 'mixer' and you've got the recipe for some wild racing. Mud racers race one a time and only one mud pit is used so that track conditions are the same for every competitor. Before competitors line up to make their pass across the pit, they are first hooked up to a long tow cable. That way, the vehicles that get stuck in the bog can get pulled out easily. If a tow cable breaks it usually takes a big excavator to retrieve the submerged mud racer. Once properly tethered, the racer will climb a short incline to get to the edge of the pit. Given the green light, the racer takes off to try to earn the lowest time to make a full pass across the mud.

The things to watch in mud racing are the launch of the vehicle, its ability to be consistent and a driver's smooth touch. Remember, too, that the first few attempts will usually result in less than a full pass. That's because the mixture is more water than dirt. When the competitors start making full passes, then it comes down to time. Every competitor gets timed and the fastest full pass for each class is the winner. The more advanced classes seem to simply glide over the mud with a highflying rooster tail of wet sloppy mud.

Doing the same thing on a level sand surface is called Sand Drags and while mud racers race one a time, Sand Drags are contested two at a time. The majority of high end, Sand Drag racers are lightweight rides that look like pavement drag cars. The 4X4 rides of sand dragging are just as exciting. Using tires that have a tread pattern that looks more like a series of paddles than tread, they use the same principal of skimming across the surface rather than lose time digging in. It all comes down to consistency, enough horsepower to work those paddle tires, and a driver's deft touch. Side-by-side racing adds to the excitement of two racers racing each other and the track. There is even uphill drag racing.

Dirt drags are very similar to sand drags in that they are contested two at a time on a flat surface. But on dirt, the four-wheel drive racers are king as four wheels, again with paddle tires, propelling the racer to a quick time are better. Much like pavement drag racing, there is a starting light device and lights that time the runs. The big difference is that dirt is less fine than sand and therefore needs to be 'worked' more to get across faster. Often, the only thing fans see in a dirt drag race is the

A relatively stock-looking Jeep takes on the mud pit and it looks like he's doing OK. But looks can be deceiving, especially when it involves six feet of wet, sloppy mud.

He's got a long and soupy way to go and now it's all about the momentum and getting up on top of the mud to get across for the best possible time.

front wheels of the racers. Regular track maintenance and grooming keeps deep grooves from forming, allowing racers to race consistently. It's not unusual to see the backhoes out after as few as two or three runs to get the track back to its original state.

Monster Trucks often drag race as part of their show. They, too, start from a dead stop and race over dirt ramps often with the finish line on the crest of the last jump. It's pretty impressive to see those Monsters high in the air, motors straining, winning a neck-to-neck race by a nose. But like the others, 4X4 drag racers race in mud, dirt or sand and they take their racing seriously.

Jus Mite, a racer with an old Chevy truck body, starts off his Mud Pit run like this: spinning his way across the top of the mud. But when he's done…

…Jus Mite looks like this. All that wet mud adds weight to the truck and that can hurt its performance by helping it to 'sink' in the wet mud instead of staying on the surface.

50

Yet, the driver is very happy he made a full pass and can continue racing towards being the winner in his class. Mud racers have numerous classes based on weight, engines and other equipment differences.

This Dodge will have some extra cleaning to do after the races. Driving through mud puts dirt in most places while spinning your tires makes sure it gets in everywhere!

This mud racer has gone the distance but he may pay the price when it comes to broken equipment. Running an engine at maximum RPM can invite weak parts to finally break down.

The big Dodge Ram Monster Truck, Ramunition, comes back to earth after jumping a ramp in a drag race. The Monsters will often race a short straightaway with a jump at the finish line in drag racing fashion.

Bigfoot takes off from a ramp during the drag portion of the show. Drag racing Monsters shows just how much horsepower it takes to move a big, 10,000 lb. truck.

Bigfoot takes off with full power and lifts the front wheels. Most Monster Trucks have enough raw horsepower to lift their heavy front wheels in acceleration much like a lighter drag car.

Bigfoot beats the Raminator across the finish line in drag competition. Note pylons with checkered flags. They need to be big so fans and drivers can see where the course ends.

This Jeep is really slingin' the mud and an aggressive attack is one way to take on the mud. Another is a consistent application of power to stay closer to the surface and avoid sinking.

Sometimes, nothing can help and the mud racer eventually sinks in and the score is Mud 1 – Racer ZERO. Now, the long pull backwards will remind the driver he didn't complete his mission. Note towrope pulling him out.

Another Jeep digs in and proves the versatility of a vehicle that was originally invented for military use. Today, a large portion of the off-road industry involves Jeeps and their many variations.

The big splash at the end is kind of hard to miss for both drivers and fans. But as it signals a full pass, it is a welcome sight to celebrate for both.

A Jeep makes its way out of the mud pit proving it's not always about bigger, heavier and more powerful 4X4s. Smaller, lighter and less powerful rides can be consistent winners, too.

Will Monster-style tires help this Ford make it all the way? It's not always about just the tires. Like any competitive vehicle, it also includes the driveline and suspension and how they are set up.

This Ford's Monster-style tires seemed to help it make it to the end of the mud pit as he is splashing his way out. Knowledgeable race fans know it takes more than just one piece of equipment to win.

Two Monster Trucks at the finish line show that even with all that horsepower, big tires and physical mass, it still comes down to who can hit the line first.

A typical dirt drag tire with 'paddles' to dig in. They are not designed to dig in and move the dirt as much as move the racer forward on the surface of the dirt.

Drag racers will often add extra weight over the axles of their racers to increase traction. Note the relocation of the battery to the rear for the same effect in this acceleration-based racing.

Rehab is a dirt drag truck made from a Ford Bronco. Note full cage with wing on top and how many components have been relocated atop the rear of the truck such as radiator and the truck's electrical shutoff.

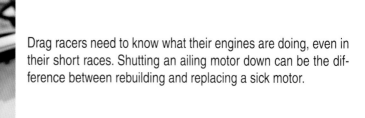

Drag racers need to know what their engines are doing, even in their short races. Shutting an ailing motor down can be the difference between rebuilding and replacing a sick motor.

This Ford is shown attacking the mud pit full on. An all out attack at the start can be enough to maintain momentum for a full pass and a win.

A Chevy truck that has been extensively modified just for mud racing takes on the pit. Additional frame clearance, suspension travel and more horsepower are the basic modifications for winning.

Wearing a fresh coat of mud, this Ford, minus a headlight, makes it out of the pit. Note the Mudbanditz logo on the windshield. Off-Roading clubs are a common sight at race events.

A big splash signals the end of the track (note cone on right) for this Chevy. It's almost like a trophy for going the distance and having a big celebration.

When the Gravelrama event is ready to commence, a four-wheel drive Jeep with a large Gravelrama sign comes down the hill to the wild applause of the large crowd of Off-Road fans.

CHAPTER 4: HILL CLIMBS

The 4x4 trucks continue to amaze with their accomplishments including the climbing of steep hills and even racing up mountains.

Hill Climbs:

The Hill Climb is another challenge to 4WD Off-Road trucks, which is similar in some aspects with the Uphill Drag competitions. But the Hill Climb takes the Uphill Drag event further. First of all, they are longer in some cases—much, much longer in others. The biggest difference between the Uphill Drags and Hill Climbs is that there is only one vehicle at a time competing in the

Hill Climbs. Also in the Uphill Drags, the two vehicles are probably accelerating as they cross the finish line. But with some of the Hill Climb competitions, the 4x4 truck may come to a halt somewhere on the course, being unable to maintain traction.

Two of the biggest Hill Climb challenges are about as different as can be imagined. One of them is man-made while the other is a magnificent product of Mother Nature.

The Big Eliminator Hill — The first is the so-called "Big Eliminator Hill" near Cleves, Ohio. It is part of a former gravel pit that sponsors an annual national off-road event called Gravelrama, and that famous hill is a 175-foot-tall pile of pea gravel!

Nobody really knows exactly the angle of the hill because it changes every year when it is rebuilt. But rest it to say that it has to be some 70 degrees or greater. Just looking at its amazing height and that seemingly near straight-up side, you have to wonder how any four-wheeled vehicle could make the ascent to the top. There have been times when a truck loses traction and, while trying to get going again, practically buries itself.

The Big Hill climb actually starts from a pit at the base of the hill. The goal is to go from a standing start at the bottom and get your truck over the top—not an easy job. The hill has defeated many of those who have challenged it. It is indeed a unique title to be a member of the "Over-The-Hill Gang."

Four-wheel-drive trucks that test the Big Hill are similar to those that do the Flat and Up Hill drags. Drivers indicated that they lowered their tire pressures to increase tire grip. Others indicated that they lowered the float level on their carburetors because of the high angle of the hill. Still one other driver said that the sensation was like "trying to get a boat up on a plane." Of course, the scooper tires are a huge advantage in grabbing those small stone pebbles.

So what happens when a number of over-the-hill trips are accomplished by a number of trucks? To solve the tie, the trucks are brought back to run again, only this time, they start a little higher on the hill making it much more difficult. If nobody goes over the top, the winner is the truck going the furthest up the hill.

Pikes Peak Hill Climb — Another variation of the up-hill competition, possibly the ultimate up-hill course, occurs at the famous Pikes Peak Hill Climb. It's a race of sorts, with both 2WD and 4x4 truck and car classes, because it does begin with a standing start and the fastest to the top is the winner. Again it's a one-at-a-time situation. A number of pickups have participated in this world-famous competition over the years.

Officially known as the Pikes Peak International

There are a number of different tire types to decide between for the hill-climbing task. Those huge protruding cleats on the tire surface provide huge pulling power in getting the 4x4 over the top of the hill.

The crowd at Gravelrama is not seated on civilized bleachers, but on the ground or folding chairs. Everybody is waiting for the first four-wheeler to give that tall pile of pea gravel its best shot.

If you don't think that the Gravelrama hill is super tall, just check the size of the people that are at the bottom. By the way, unlike the uphill drags, the hill climb does it one vehicle at a time.

Hill Climb (PPIHC), unofficially it's 'The Race to the Clouds' and it requires the climbing of this 4,721-foot mountain. There are 156 turns on grades averaging seven percent over both gravel and paved sections of road. It has taken place for over 90 years and there is a class for just about every type of vehicle. There are a number of classes that allow 4x4 trucks including Pro Trucks (tube frame, off-road trucks with a stock external appearance) and Pikes Peak Open Trucks that look like a stock vehicle but retain little of the original design.

The changing road surfaces running to the summit are a significant challenge because the truck can't be configured for a single surface. The first three miles of the course are pavement, followed by three miles of dirt, then it's back to pavement for another three miles, with the final race to the top being dirt. But there is also one other characteristic of this unique course, the start isn't at the bottom of the mountain, but actually seven miles past that point.

Of course, the biggest aspect that has to be addressed by this Pikes Peak challenge is tire selection. Obviously, there has to be a compromise between dirt and pavement configurations. To cover the distance to the top, the times usually vary between 12 and 15 minutes. It's a real workout and you're ready to kick back on completion of the run to the clouds.

Chad Larsen of Loudenville, Ohio, owns this '88 Chevy S-10 hill climb truck. He's made it up the Big Hill six times in this $12,000 truck. It's powered by a modified 350-cubic-inch V-8 capable of about 500 horsepower. It's got a stripped-out interior that has only the essentials including a racing seat, internal roll cage, tach, and gauges. Wouldn't you agree that this is a very economical way to go off-roading?

John Pruitt of Milan, Indiana, owns this 1993 Chevy Blazer. Costing $32,000 to build, Pruitt indicated, "It will last forever." He also indicated that on the Gravelrama Hill, he lowered the tire pressure for more traction. It uses two types of tires, the expected paddle wheels on the rear and less-radical ribbed tires on the front. You can see that the Blazer has been stripped of much of its weight leaving just what is needed. The final photo shows the Family Tradition, powered by its 383 cid carbureted engine, going over the top in an earlier Big Hill run.

One of the most famous runs up the Gravelrama hill took place a number of years ago when the most famous 4x4 truck, Bigfoot, gave it a good shot. Partially up the hill, those huge front tires came off the ground.

Some 4x4 trucks pound over the top of the Big Hill while others labor at the end trying to make it. It appears that this truck is in the latter category as there is still gravel being thrown by the left rear tire.

This head-on shot shows a Chevy pickup challenging Pike's Peak. It's being driven by Jack Flannery during the 1991 event. The 4x4 truck carries a number of protective bars on the front.

This 2003 Chevy S-10 extended cab pickup, driven by David Schmidt in the 2007 event, displays excellent traction on the dirt portion of the Pikes Peak course. The truck is certainly noticeable with its showcar looks.

Glen Harris pounds down the power on his 1988 run up the Pikes Peak incline. Pulling a quick right turn, the B-2600 Mazda 4x4 truck shows the front tires making a considerable contribution in traction.

Rob Reinerston is shown blowing his left-rear tire racing up the mountain during the 2008 Pikes Peak Hill Climb. His 4x4 truck is a 2006 Ford F-150. The popularity of the Pikes Peak event is verified by the number of photographers in the background.

A big sky is the background for Leanard Vahsholtz in his 2005 Ford Explorer. Look at the small hills of dust coming off the left front tire. The 2008 effort of 11:44.32 was good for a course record in its class.

Beautiful rock formations serve as the back-drop for Bill Mears' run up the mountain. The bright red truck is a nearly stock Dodge pickup. Its tune was an impressive 15:17.40 clocking.

Even the semis with their four rear tandems of wheels like to give the big mountain a shot. This streamlined CFI Kenworth tandem axle set-up, with Glenn Brown at the wheel, is competing in the 1999 event.

Some of the PP competitors run only a portion of the course. This 1997 Freightliner was on such a run with driver Mike Ryan behind the wheel. The time for the big rig was a 6:05.03 effort.

In 2000, Bruce Canepa wheeled his 2000 Kenworth up the Peak in 14:34.41 setting a new record (L). But time marches on and in 2003, with a new red Kenworth T2000, he bettered his previous record effort by almost 12 seconds.

Almost there! A specially built hill climber is just about ready to crest his hill. Note the front wheels coming off the dirt and the rear tires still digging in. He's close to hitting his max for acceleration and weight transfer.

The High Roller Modified 4WD truck demonstrates clearly the all-wheel drive capabilities of its powertrain. The dirt can be seen swirling from the two front tires, and it's coming off at even a greater intensity from the rears.

CHAPTER 5: PULLING

Pulling is a competition where 4x4 trucks are very popular, a sport where speed isn't the key requirement. Here, it's having brute power and the ability to put it to the track. The goal of the sport is to pull a giant weight, called a sled, as far as possible down a three-hundred-foot dirt track. The run starts off with very little weight to pull, but as the distance down the track increases, the weight increases, making forward progress more and more difficult.

Pickup Pulling Trucks:

Pickup trucks are somewhat of a recent edition to the pulling sport, which started in the beginning with tractors. But with the addition of the pickup classes in the early 1980s, they have become one of the top pulling fan draws. In all the classes, there is the battle of the different brands, which is one of the high points of this competition to the middle America crowds that attend these events.

These four-wheelers with their four giant cleated tires extending far beyond the constraints of the body sheet metal are brutish-looking machines that pound down the track with dirt flowing from all four wheels. Engines for the 4x4 pulling trucks are monstrous big blocks that produce huge torque and horsepower.

But it's not only horsepower that is required to pull that huge weight that minimal distance. Here, it's torque that the engines are designed to produce. Most of the

Another view of the power of the NTPA 4x4 Modified trucks. With big power and traction required coming off the starting line, it's clear from the rear of this truck that requirement is definitely being accomplished.

weight of these trucks comes in the form of heavy steel weights that are hung far out in front of the vehicle. There is no suspension on the rear of the chassis as the rear axle is physically attached to the frame. In the front, there is pretty standard suspension with coil springs and shocks. Special cleated tires are used to drive these machines down the track. Their tall cleats have been cut down so only a fine edge remains.

Getting momentum as quickly as possible is the name of the game here as the weight is at its lightest at the start of the pull. Following are the three basic types of 4x4 pulling pickup trucks and what makes them tick:

Carbureted 4x4 Pulling Pickup Trucks — This base truck type uses a carbureted V-8 engine to push the power to the wheels. They go by different names across the country, but the trucks used by the Midsouth Pullers (called Pro-Stock 4WD Trucks) are pretty typical of the class. To keep the cost down, a steel 472 cid engine (with the exception of an aluminum intake) and a 750 cfm carburetor are used. Horsepower is in the 800-horse range. Interestingly, the truck must carry a windshield, back glass, and the stock steel body. Chevy S-10s and Ford Rangers are the popular brands. The trucks run in the 6200-pound weight class and can serve as a starting point for first-time pullers.

It's not uncommon in the NTPA Modified 4x4 Truck Class to see old body shells over the chassis. It certainly doesn't add or subtract from the performance of the truck, but they are certainly a crowd pleaser. Just check out this old *Half Century* truck.

Modified 4x4 Pulling Pickup Trucks — The so-called Modified Trucks are very similar to the carbureted-engine trucks with the exception of fuel injection replacing carburetors. These engines are capable of providing four-figure horsepower outputs from their 650-cubic-inch powerplants. This style of pulling truck can usually be identified by the twin exhaust stacks that protrude above the engine. As in other four-wheel-drive classes, the engine is mounted forward of its factory position.

Super-Modified 4x4 Pulling Pickup Trucks — The point should be made on these trucks that they are practically identical to the Modified 4WD Trucks, only these trucks are powered by supercharged powerplants. Even though these engines are smaller than their Modified brothers, they are capable of over 2000 horsepower from 500-cubic-inch engines. Many of these trucks mount the largest 14.71 superchargers on their engines. And if that wasn't enough power, most of the top 4WD Super Mod Pullers had their massive blowers overdriven as much as 50 percent! Driving the Super Modified trucks is much more critical than with the less powerful trucks. Drivers explained that it is more difficult to get all that power hooked up to the track. With that additional power, there is a tendency to have wheel-spin if you get into the throttle just a little too hard.

The Killer Modified 4wd Truck was a strong competitor in the southern United States. Notice the forward rake of the truck and the front wheels mounted completely outside the bodylines. And how about those mean eyes staring at you from the front weight box?

Diesel 4x4 Pulling Pickup Trucks — In recent years, a new type of 4x4 pulling truck has started making itself known in the sport. Introduced by the Diesel Hot Rod Association, the diesel four-wheeler powerplants can really put the power down. These trucks also use water injection to increase horsepower. There have been several classes in diesel pulling, including Street Diesel, Pro-Street, and Modified Diesel. The rules also limit the engine blocks to those available for each brand of truck. These diesel engines spool up like a conventional diesel engine and suddenly blast out a huge column of black smoke. The distinctive whistle fans hear comes not from a supercharger, but from a turbocharger that will make that noise when enough air is forced through it. Again, with the number of diesel trucks being built, the popularity of this class will continue to grow.

Semi Truck 4x4 Pullers — The idea of introducing a monster semi truck into the pulling sport was considered crazy in many quarters. But the spectacle of a brightly painted 20,000 lb. Peterbilt or Kenworth chugging to the line and puffing out those columns of smoke, has an attraction all its own. Maybe it's that characteristic rumble that only a semi can generate, or the brand recognition factor the fans have with the rigs they see running up and down the freeway. Whatever it is, these heavy haulers are getting quite a cult following. And when you think about it, these semis could be described as a type of four-wheel-drive pullers. There is, however, one difference in the location of the pulling tires with these all located together behind the cab. The configuration is actually four tandems of two tires each. Those dual tires each work together as one, giving the same effect as four pulling tires.

This is a rather menacing view of a Modified pulling 4x4 truck coming right at you. Notice that the driver is sitting near the center of the interior. The success of a pull is largely dependent on how well those front wheels are locked to the track.

The Wildfire is giving the sled a wild ride in this summer NTPA pull. Clearly visible are the driveline from the transfer case and the custom frame. The stands are packed for many of these events as can be seen at this particular event.

The XTreme 4x4 Modified pulling truck of RB Moler is shown in a 2003 pull. The truck has showcar looks with its green flames cascading back on the body sides. Also notice the height of the injected powerplant.

The 3 Bears Modified 4x4 pulling truck was one of the NTPA's most recognizable trucks for many years. If you look closely, you can see one of those bears riding in the passenger seat.

No mistaking the look of a Supermodified 4x4 pulling truck engine. The supercharger sits atop the engine intake and the drive pulley sits in front of it. Finally, there are the butterfly valves on top of the blower which open when the engine is running.

Here's a shot of another Supermod powerplant. This particular engine has a protective shield about the blower belt. The short vertical exhaust pipes are indicative of this type of blown powerplant.

The Fantasy 4WD Super Modified pulling truck is powering down the track at an NTPA national pull. No doubt from that bowtie bumper that this is a Chevy truck. Notice that the fuel tank is mounted directly in front of the grille.

The Bad Habit Super Modified 4x4 puller has color-coated the top of the engine with its dark yellow body color. It appears to be a very 'heavy' track that the Bad Habit is testing.

The weight box of this Super Modified four-wheeler provides a great location to display its Super Chevy name and Superman logo. The 4x4 Super Modified trucks are one of NTPA's most popular classes.

Although the age of this 4x4 Super Modified Truck numbers in the decades, it still makes an interesting puller. The Bone truck powered down the track with all four wheels contributing to the momentum shown here.

Diesel power combined with a four-wheel-drive powertrain makes for a super-effective pulling truck. It's obvious that there is a huge contribution being made by the powerplant of this attractive 4x4 diesel pulling truck.

There has always been an attraction to the Super Stock diesel Tractors with their large column of black smoke billowing skyward. Now, that same spectacle is available from a 4x4 pulling truck.

When the National Tractor Pulling Association (NTPA) showcased its huge Bowling Green, Ohio, pulling event in 2004, it used a 4x4 Modified pulling truck on the advertisement. The big 4X4s are one of the more popular attractions in pulling.

With so many of the newer and larger pickups carrying diesel powerplants, adding a pulling class just for them made sense. Also, these engines produce a different sound from the other engines.

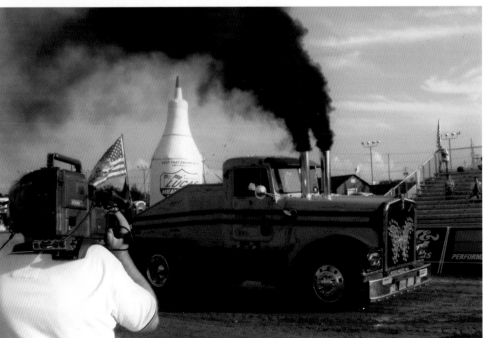

The Semi Pullers are a real fan favorite. With their four tandem wheels pulling together, they are basically a four-wheeler, but their four tandems are located on the rear of the trucks. This is the famous truck of JR Collins, one of the top semi pullers in the 2000s.

It's an amazing sight to view one of these pulling semis pounding down the pulling track with those two exhaust stacks emitting columns of black smoke. Needless to say, the amount of weight pulled by these giant machines is the most of any pulling vehicle.

The engines for these semi pullers aren't changed to any great extent. The increase in power comes from the increase in the fuel/air mixture with the addition of multiple turbochargers. The engine in the red JR Collins truck has almost 1000 cubic inches, 2600 horsepower, and 4 large turbochargers.

This photo provides a view of one of the four wheels (actually two wheels in each tandem acting as a single wheel). Unlike other forms of racing, the more wheels on the racing surface, the better the traction.

There is huge torque load available from these large turbo-charged powerplants. It is easy to see that here with the left front wheel lifted. Much like drag racing, when weight transfer meets torque, the chassis can lift the front end.

As strange as it might seem for a 4x4 pulling truck, you might think that there should be equal weight front and rear. Not the case, though, since a vast majority is carried up front in the form of massive steel blocks.

The 4x4 pulling truck is also unique in its suspension system. First, there is the rear of the truck where this NO suspension is totally solid. Up front are coil springs such as these shown here.

The 4x4 pulling trucks haven't been around nearly as long as the two-wheel-drive pulling truck shown here. The types are as different as night and day. It's not uncommon to see two-wheelers pull wheelies as shown here, something that you would never see with a four-wheeler.

With the huge power and torque provided by the big block engines, a strong frame is a necessity. This is an example of the tubular frames that the four-wheel pulling trucks require.

No mistaking the look of a 4x4 pulling truck coming at you head-on. Note that the cleated front tires reach out far beyond the body's sheet metal constraints. It's easy to see that those front tires are providing traction to aid in the pull.

This engine is typical of the type used in the carbureted engine classes. Although, they don't make the power of the injected and supercharged engines, these powerplants still make enough power to provide entertaining pulling competition.

It's really amazing how far that front weight box hangs out in front of the grille. That's the situation for any type of 4x4 pulling truck, no matter what type of powerplant is sitting under the hood.

A highly modified Jeep takes on a rock crawl. Note the lighter color control arms of the suspension. The longer than stock bars allow for more suspension travel and chassis clearance.

CHAPTER 6. ROCK CRAWLING AND TRAIL RIDES

Racing 4X4s is intense and powerful and a few of the lesser known aspects of the sport also share those traits. But they use their power and intensity in a very different way. Rock Crawling and Trail Rides have seen a surge in popularity and for the same reasons as other 4X4 sports—they're fun!

Rock Climbing takes the power aspect and turns it around to do the almost impossible: traversing mounds of jagged rocks without doing any damage to vehicle or driver. The key to winning here is slow and safe. To do that, the driver uses his vehicle's suspension to the maximum, gauging each rock and boulder to ensure enough clearance to pass. Like Tough Trucks, it's an obstacle course of sorts, and the first object is the make it across. Also like Tough Trucks, the new guys quickly find out that momentum can help or hurt one's progress. It's one thing to have a 4X4 with enough ground clearance to clear a rock. But having a dip under one wheel can mean

the frame, or worse yet, the oil pan, transmission or even the radiator, can come slamming down on a sharp rock instead of the usual soft dirt or mud found in off-roading. It doesn't take a viewer of Rock Climbing long to recognize the sickening 'thunk' of a transmission or other vital component hitting a rock with disastrous results. It usually signals game over and then it's time for the really big tow truck to come in and remove the damaged carcass.

So the idea for these slow and smart racers is to pick an imaginary plane across the tops of the rocks and drive it. When there is a dip or a climb to deal with, the driver's eyes and brain quickly study what the other side of the vehicle will be driving on. Will it be enough to clear the frame or allow the wheels to make progress? When the driver rolls down off that peak, will the rear suspension clear the rocks? You might be able to take the front of the racer over a particularly sharp rock but what about the middle and back?

Rock Climbing courses will often have two runs with one being more difficult than the other. The tougher of the two may look intimidating to those thinking of even walking across it. It's like a multi-level chess game and for many, very complicated. Articulating suspension with huge amounts of travel, guessing how your racer will span multiple formations, what goes up must come down, all while trying to keep moving to get a good time and win.

Trail Rides are similar but use bigger, more open areas, sometimes crossing miles instead of feet. The 4X4s run one at a time or single file, letting the first racer cross a difficult area first before heading into it themselves. They are also running an obstacle course but it's more of a natural one. They may run, sometimes literally, into a natural mud pit of a river or creek bottom. They may have a hard time making it up or down a hill safely. And trying to pass on a path that is narrower than your 4X4 is always tricky. Yet, Trail Riding is more for just fun than competition. Yes, after the excursion, the winner may get to do some bragging but mostly it's about fun for all as others are riding along for the trip.

Trail Riders may often have only small areas of rock to clear. They are more inclined to cross small streams and rivers only to find out the surface under the water is anything less then level. Drop two wheels into a downhill crevice, underwater or not, and there's a good chance your 4X4 is going to tip over. Unlike Rock Crawling, winches are a big part of Trail Riding and come in very handy in areas where a local tow truck is not going to make house calls.

Rock Crawling and Trail Riding is all about power but instead of horsepower and throwing a 4X4 over a ramp and gaining valuable seconds, it's about the torque that gets a 4X4 over a big rock—even if it is one wheel at a time. It's about using four-wheel drive to cross that riverbed instead of sinking into it forever. And while brute force and horsepower can be entertaining, it's mostly about getting where you want to go smoothly and safely for a change.

A specially built rock crawler does its thing. Note the extreme articulation between the front axle and the rear. It's needed to clear the highs and lows of a rock course.

From the side, you can see just how much clearance is needed to cross the mountain of jagged rocks that can project up as well as create a deep hole for a wheel to cross.

When you make a successful run with a rock crawler, you can celebrate with a 'Crab Walk' using your same four-wheel steering that allows you to maneuver the rocks deftly.

With a tire on the edge of one rock and another tire off the ground completely, this rock-crawling Jeep is running out of options. But rock crawling is about perseverance more than horsepower.

With the truck up to the rocker panels in rock, this crawler is running out of choices. In rock crawling, there comes a point when the vehicle can get 'trapped' between rocks and cannot move anywhere.

This rock crawler was stripped of excess weight because any good racer runs better when lighter. Lighter racers are more maneuverable and that helps the driver use the vehicle's weight to his advantage.

It may start off with only one or two rocks to negotiate, but things will get more complicated as all four wheels have to work together instead of fighting one another for movement.

In trail riding, things can get pretty narrow for a 4X4 and that's part of the attraction. It's not unusual to meet a trail the riders have never seen before and have to learn quickly.

This Jeep rock climber and obstacle racer is all set with a roll cage that completely protects the body. The big crawling tires are more about grip than moving dirt or mud. A long shock/strut means longer suspension travel and a better ability to climb rocks.

With some of the rocks reaching past the centerline of this Jeep's axles, it could become rough going pretty quickly for this rock crawler. Once an obstacle passes the centerline of the axles, it becomes a threat to bottoming out and stalling the forward progress of the vehicle.

Notice how close the truck's front axle is to a rock that could cause plenty of damage. A rock-crawling driver has to feel and know where his critical components are on every inch of a tough course.

RESOURCES

<u>4x4 Truck Magazines:</u>
Off-Road
4-Wheel & Off-Road
Four Wheeler
Dusty Times

<u>Off-Road Associations:</u>
CORR, Championship Off-Road Racing, corracing.com
SCORE, International Road Racing, score-international.com
SNORE, Southern Nevada Off-Road Enthusiasts, snoreracing.net
BITD, Best in the Desert, bitd@worldnet.att.net
MDR, Mojave Desert Racing, mdrracing@aol.com

<u>Sand/Dirt Drag Organizations:</u>
ASRO, American Sand Racing Organization, asro.com
EC4WDA, East Coast 4-wheel Association, ec4wda.org
GLFWDA, Great Lakes 4-Wheel Drive Association, glfda@voyager.net
M4x4, Montana 4x4 Association, mcm.net
MSRA, Missouri Sand Racing Association, angelfire.com
NWSCA, Northwest Sand Competition Association, sandrail.com
Old Dominion 4-Wheel Drive Club, bodatious.com
OOHVA, Oregon Off-Highway Vehicle Association, webmaster@oohva.org
PNWAWDA, Pacific Northwest 4-Wheel Drive Association, off-road.com
SSDRA, Sand Sports Drag Racing Association, mearsracing.com
SWFWDA, Southwest 4-Wheel Drive Association, 4x4now.com
UFWDA, United 4-Wheel Drive, ufwda.org
West Tennessee Sand Drags, geocities.com

<u>Hill Climb Organizations:</u>
PPHC, Pikes Peak Hill Climb, pphc.com
gravelrama, Gravelrama.com

<u>Mud Racing Associations:</u>
MSMRA, Mid-States Mud Race Association, msmrs.com
NMRA, National Mud Racing Association
NMBA, National Mud Bog Association, http://national mudbogassociation.com
HMRA, Hometown Mud Racing Association, hmra.org

<u>Truck Pulling Associations:</u>
Big Rigs Pulling Series, bigrigspulling.com
NTPA, National Tractor Pulling Association, ntpapull.com
Outlaw Pullers Association, outlawhotrodpullers.com
OTPPA, Outlaw Truck and Tractor Pullers Association, Outlawpulling.com
DHRA, Diesel Hot Rod Association, dhraonline.com

<u>Monster Truck Associations:</u>
USHRA, US Hot Rod Association, ushra.com
The Promotion Company/Special Events, familyevents.com
Bigfoot4x4, Inc., bigfoot4x4.com
MTRA, Monster Truck Racing Association, mtra.us

<u>Rockcrawler Organizations:</u>
RCAA, Rock Crawlers Association of America, rockcrawler.org
UROC Pro National Series, uroc.com
Black Hills 4-Wheelers, bh4wheelers.com
CalROCS Series, California Rock-Crawling Off-Road Championship Series, calrocs.com

RACING

RECREATIONAL VEHICLES & OTHER

TRUCKS

More Great Titles From
Iconografix

All Iconografix books are available from direct mail specialty book dealers and bookstores worldwide, or can be ordered from the publisher. For book trade and distribution information or to add your name to our mailing list and receive a **FREE CATALOG** contact:

Iconografix, Inc.
PO Box 446, Dept BK
Hudson, WI, 54016

Telephone: (715) 381-9755, (800) 289-3504 (USA), Fax: (715) 381-9756
info@iconografixinc.com
www.iconografixinc.com

More great books from
Iconografix

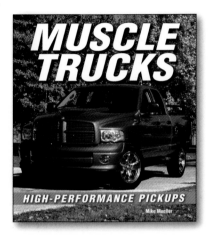

ISBN 978-1-58388-197-2

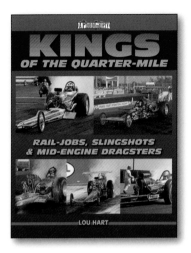

ISBN 978-1-58388-234-4

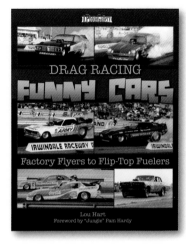

ISBN 978-1-58388-220-7

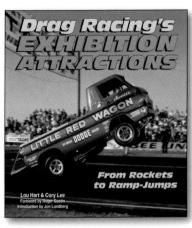

ISBN 978-1-58388-208-5

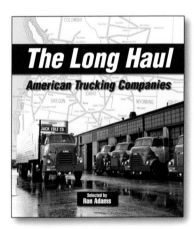

ISBN 978-1-58388-211-5

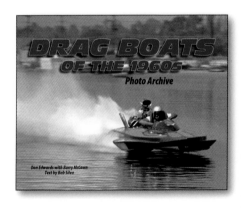

ISBN 978-1-58388-222-1

Iconografix, Inc.
P.O. Box 446, Dept BK,
Hudson, WI 54016
For a free catalog call: 1-800-289-3504
info@iconografixinc.com
www.iconografixinc.com

More Great Titles From
Iconografix

All Iconografix books are available from direct mail specialty book dealers and bookstores worldwide, or can be ordered from the publisher. For book trade and distribution information or to add your name to our mailing list and receive a **FREE CATALOG** contact:

Iconografix, Inc.
PO Box 446, Dept BK
Hudson, WI, 54016

Telephone: (715) 381-9755, (800) 289-3504 (USA), Fax: (715) 381-9756
info@iconografixinc.com
www.iconografixinc.com

*This product is sold under license from Mack Trucks, Inc. Mack is a registered Trademark of Mack Trucks, Inc. All rights reserved.

More great books from
Iconografix

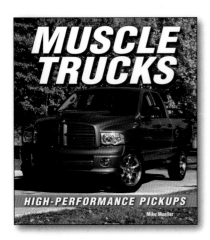
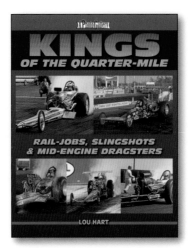
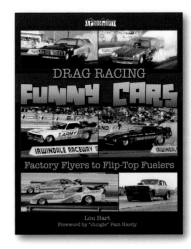
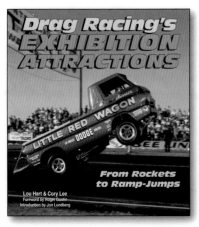
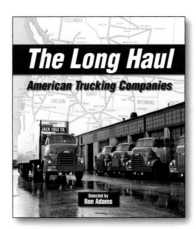
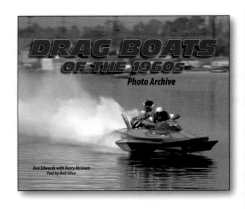
Iconografix, Inc.
P.O. Box 446, Dept BK,
Hudson, WI 54016
For a free catalog call: 1-800-289-3504
info@iconografixinc.com
www.iconografixinc.com